THE
BOOK
OF
LIGHT

365 ways to bring light into your life

MIKAELA KATHERINE JONES

Conari Press

This edition first published in 2018 by Conari Press, an imprint of Red Wheel/
Weiser, LLC
With offices at:
65 Parker Street, Suite 7
Newburyport, MA 01950
www.redwheelweiser.com

ISBN: 978-1-57324-730-6
Library of Congress Cataloging-in-Publication Data available upon request.

Cover design by Kathryn Sky-Peck with special thanks to Nate Jensen
Interior by Jane Hagaman
Typeset in Adobe Caslon

Printed in Canada
MAR
10 9 8 7 6 5 4 3 2 1

The advice published in this book is presented without guarantee of outcome.
Readers using the information in this book do so entirely at their own risk and the
author and publisher accept no liability if adverse effects are caused.

To all of my brothers and sisters,

who are committed to shining your light

with the world . . . no matter what.

Thank you.

Dear Reader,

You are a magnificent, spiritual being of Light, blessed with many innate gifts, which you are here to express. Remember this. You are here to make a positive contribution to the world, and you are deserving of deep love, joy and fulfillment. These are your divine birthrights.

Living an awakened, deeply fulfilling life doesn't happen overnight. It takes practice. Daily practice. This book is not just a "book." It is a beam of light that holds great transformative power. Don't be fooled by its simple title—it's not just a collection of "airy fairy" ideas for how to be happy. Each "Way" offers a practical suggestion or nugget of inspiration that will help bring you clarity and peace of mind, help you live from the wisdom of your heart, and help you fully embody the Light that you are.

Read from the book daily. Use it as part of your meditation practice. Ask yourself, "How can I bring more light into my life?" or, "How can I live from my Light?" Then randomly open to and read one of the passages. Or start from the beginning and proceed forward daily. The 365 ways to bring light into your life will help you to be your most empowered, true self each day of the year. And when you consistently practice with an open heart and mind, your life will shine. And you, in your own unique way, will be a lighthouse of peace, love, and delight.

—With boundless love and appreciation
for the light that you are,
Mikaela

365 Ways
to Bring Light
into Your Life

1

Listen to the calm, peaceful voice inside you. It's the voice of your heart, which is the most illuminated voice in your life. Close your eyes, take a few slow, deep breaths, and place your hands on your heart. Ask if it has a message for you in this moment. It may be as simple as a word or a feeling. Surrender and trust it.

2

Step into yourself. Become the YOU, you always intended to be. You have a beautiful gift to give. What excites you? What lights you up? Follow your joy, and your presence will be a gift to the world.

3

Call on the angels. Ask for their love and guidance. They are always available to help you. If you ask, you will receive their love and wisdom in their unique, joyful, and often humorous ways.

4

Take time to relax every day.

Honor it as you would an appointment.

Listen to some music.

Take a walk.

Do some deep breathing
or roll around on the floor and stretch.

5

Send love to as many people as you can today. It's easy. Simply think, "I send you love" to everyone you see. Or if you don't physically see them, picture them in your mind's eye and send them a loving thought.

6

Commit to an art form. Your art may be dancing, singing, or writing. Or it may be raising healthy children with strong self-esteem. It could be saving Mother Earth or helping the homeless. And it may change over time. Whatever it is, commit, and your fulfillment in life will blossom.

7

Quantum physics shows us that at the deepest level, we are all connected. By choosing to live by your powerful loving light, you bring light to the whole world. Thank you.

8

Bring natural elements into your home. Plants and flowers will help clean the air and nourish your soul. Save the pinecones, rocks, and shells you find. Add them to your altar or mantel. Adding nature to your surroundings will anchor you with feelings of peace and well-being.

9

Give up your need to be perfect. As long as you're in your body, you still have things to learn and experience. The goal is not to be perfect, it's to express your light.

10

Eat dark chocolate. Every day. Yes! Just a square or two. Preferably raw. Chocolate is chock-full of phytonutrients, powerful plant nutrients that improve your mood and boost your energy.

11

Visualize what you'd like to create in your life. Be specific. Try to feel how it would feel to have it or be it. The energy of exhilaration you conjure through this practice will bring it into reality.

12

Practice grounding. Place your bare feet upon the grass, dirt, sand, or concrete for some time every day. Whether you walk, sit, or lie upon the earth, you will receive her energy, stabilize your nervous system, and boost your immunity.

13

The universe will support you in achieving your highest potential. Sometimes it might feel like a hug or look like a high five, sometimes it might feel like a sidestep or look like a scowl. Trust that all the signs are pointing you further down the path of your deepest fulfillment.

14

Hang a wind chime outside of the room where you spend the most time. The sound of the chime can have a powerful effect on your nervous system. It can help you to think creatively and clearly and soothe and uplift you.

15

Before you make any important actions or decisions, check in with your higher self, your inner light. Play out the different scenarios in your mind and see which one feels best to you. It may not make the most sense, but if it feels right, trust it.

16

Make compassion your intention for the day,

your intention for your life,

your intention for eternity.

17

Practice toning, the vocalization of a single tone or vowel sound. Toning is an ancient sacred practice for health and awakening. Take a deep breath and on the exhale, sound the vowel "Ah. . . ." Hold the tone until you've fully exhaled, then repeat. Try this exercise with all of the vowel sounds to align with the deep vibrations of your soul and spirit.

18

Practice gratitude. Appreciate all that you've had, all that you have now, all that you are, all that you are becoming, and all that will come to you. Be grateful for all of it. Even the challenges. Something good comes from them, too.

19

Allow others to have their feelings of anger or pain. Be a witness by creating space for their feelings, but stay centered in your own light without taking on their emotions. Offer a shoulder, a hand, a smile, a hug. Give support, that's usually all that people want.

20

Have faith that God's future plans for you far exceed your present circumstances. Take comfort in the idea that you are exactly where you need to be at this moment in time.

21

Expand your vision. When you're working on fulfilling a goal, imagine what it would look like on a larger scale. Do you want to help the homeless in your community? Imagine your organization spreading nationwide. Your vision will help propel you forward. Imagine the possibilities.

22

Clean house. Commit to taking some time to make your home clean and tidy. Pick up, sweep, or vacuum. Clean the bathroom. Do the dishes. Put fresh sheets on your bed. Cleaning your home will clear the clutter from your mind and make room for inspiration.

23

Smile as big and as often as you are moved to! You are a beacon of light for others to remember their own capacity for joy. Be a lighthouse.

24

Honor the Divine Feminine within by embracing your capacity for compassion and deep intuition. Honor this sacred energy, and you will cultivate more creativity, connection, and community in your life.

25

When you need clarity, take a step back and seek a larger perspective. Take a walk. Go for a hike. Stand on a mountaintop.

26

Call your loved ones, especially your romantic partner, by their given name at least once a day. Research shows that couples and families who address their loved ones by their name at least once a day have longer-lasting and more fulfilling relationships.

27

Consume lots of fresh green leafy vegetables. Remember learning about photosynthesis? Or, as I used to think of it, how plants eat light? Dark greens, like kale, spinach, collards, and broccoli are powerhouses of light energy for your body.

28

Speak up for yourself—even in the smallest of ways. When you speak up for yourself in small ways, you'll find it easier to speak up for yourself in big ways too.

29

Connect with nature through your sense of touch. Feel the velvet texture of a flower's petals against your cheek. The warm beach sand between your toes. The rough bark of a tree. Physical connection with nature can restore your connection to and strengthen your inner light.

30

Your time is precious; make it your own. Be intentional with how you spend your days, especially your free time. Don't dwindle it away. Be mindful and focus your time on fulfilling your purpose, expressing your creativity, and nourishing your body and relationships.

31

You don't need anyone's approval to follow your vision. You are an expression of Divine Light. Your vision is worthy and holy. When you stay focused on this, the naysayers of the world can't keep you from manifesting your dream.

32

Create a little altar in your home. Place a candle, pictures, or statues of your spiritual teachers or finds from nature upon it. An altar is a reminder of the sacredness and beauty of life. Light the candle and express reverence daily.

33

Think before you act. We often jump to conclusions or ride on a runaway train of thought. Before you begin something new, take a moment to tune inside. Take a deep breath. Be still. Begin with thoughtful intention.

34

Let go of regrets. Reframe them as valuable lessons, lessons that have built your character and increased your capacity for compassion with others.

35

Tell your friends how much
you love and appreciate them.
Don't text them, *tell* them.

36

We all have angel guides. Call upon them. They may appear to you as spheres of light or winged beings that radiate light. Ask them if they'd like to be addressed by a certain name. Your angels are always available to help you fulfill your highest potential.

37

There is great manifestation power in your spoken
word. More power than your thoughts. Spend the day
speaking only positive, encouraging words to yourself
and others. Repeat this tomorrow.

38

Break free and let go of how you *should* act. Lead
with your heart and don't worry about what others
may think. With your heart as your guide, trust that
your actions serve the higher good.

39

Engage in a repetitive activity. Walk, weed your garden, chop vegetables, paint, or dance. Keeping your body busy will quiet your mind and connect you to your light. Your intuition will shine through.

40

Get a pet. Even if it's a little fish. Taking care of another living being adds radiance to your life.

41

Ask your inner light, "What would you have me do today?" Follow the winding path of your divine inspiration. You might find flowers where you thought there were only weeds and windows where you thought there were only walls.

42

Place sacred symbols in places where you can see them often. The symbol for peace, Om, the Lotus—whatever feels sacred to you. Symbols are powerful representations of meaning and viewing them often will have a positive effect on your wellbeing.

43

Take a digital detox.

Take breaks every day from your phone,
your computer, and your television.

Go analog.

Read a book.

Write in a journal.

Meet with a friend face to face.

44

Release your expectations. Set your intention and give gratitude in advance. Do your best, but be unattached to the results. Trust in the universe.

45

Drink lots of pure water. Water is a carrier of light. Water also flushes the toxins and waste out of your body, promotes clear thinking, and gives you energy. Refreshment and rejuvenation are just a tall, cool glass of water away.

46

You don't need to learn anything more or become anything more than you already are to make a difference in the world. Your energy, your light and your love are enough.

47

Consider supporting your health with a probiotic. A probiotic populates your gut with healthy, helpful bacteria that help keep your immune system strong, which keeps you feeling powerful.

48

Use your creativity to make tasks more enjoyable. Dishes need washing? Imagine you're washing them for the Dalai Lama. You'll be awash with feelings of reverence and honor. Stuck in traffic? Be grateful for having a car that takes you to your loved ones and to all of your favorite places. Change gears and change your mind.

49

Emotions are energy in motion. Step into the emotion of what you'd like to experience. Feel the freedom of making enough income. Feel the fulfillment in sharing your gifts. Feel the gratitude of living in a world of peace.

50

Discover your purpose.

What are your gifts?

What do you love?

How can you make a positive contribution to the world?

Listen to your light, declare it, and take action.

51

Embrace your inherent playful nature.

Go to the park.

Roll in the grass.

Make a daisy chain and give it to a stranger.

Expand your root (1st) chakra. Visualize a beautiful vortex of deep rose red light at the base of your spine. Take a few deep breaths and imagine the vortex getting bigger and brighter with each breath. The root chakra governs your physical health as well as your sense of being grounded and safe.

53

When you are feeling low, one of the quickest ways to raise your vibration is to help someone else. Get out and interact with others. Offer a helping hand, a kind word, or a hug.

54

Send yourself love every day. Look in the mirror and say, "I respect you and I love you. By the way, you're pretty awesome too."

55

Connect with your inner stillness. It's always there. Close your eyes and take a few deep breaths. Release all thought as you exhale. As thoughts arise, release them by focusing on your breath. Practice this at least once a day.

56

Get involved. Volunteer at your local hospital, animal shelter, or food bank. Those who take action in their community feel more optimistic and fulfilled.

57

Dance. Let go and be free. There is great magic in surrendering to your body's movement. Spontaneous, improvisational movement silences the left brain, the logical, factual part of our brain, and gives acceptance, wisdom, and love a chance to shine through.

58

You are so much more than your body and your personality. You are more than all of your wildest hopes and dreams. You are Infinite. Magnificent. Complete.

59

Grow a garden. Or tend to a few potted plants. Talk or sing to them so they feel your presence and care. This small act can lift your mood lift and help you grow!

60

Celebrate a member of your family today. What are your favorite qualities about this person? What are some of your favorite memories with them? Write them a note of appreciation, call them and tell them, or give them a small gift.

61

Life is not a collection of things. Life is a stream of experiences, of moments. You are free to choose how you will experience and respond to each moment. Tune into the light in your heart and you'll always choose wisely.

62

Shake it out. Whenever you feel anxious or nervous, shake out your arms and legs. Bounce up and down on your toes. Move the energy out of your body. Take a few deep breaths and return to your center.

63

Surrender to your life as it is. This does not mean you give up on your hopes and dreams, but stop focusing on how you think life *should* look. Through acceptance, your heart will open, and you will connect with your Higher Self. You will be empowered to take a step toward fulfilling your dreams.

64

Perspective reigns supreme. If you're feeling bad, shift your perspective. You have the freedom to choose how you look at life. "I didn't get the job," or "I'm never good enough," can become "I did my best. I'll do better next time," or "I know the best position for me is on its way."

65

Practice chanting the ancient Sanskrit mantra: "Om" (AUM). Chanting helps ground and center you. Chanting "Om" is believed to connect you with the wisdom of the Universe.

66

Try a fast. Drink as much water and nourishing herbal tea as you can to keep your hunger at bay. Giving your digestive system a break enables your body to repair and replenish and can even help you look and feel brighter.

67

Learn to be present with others. Really listen. Don't just think about what you're going to say next. People know when they've been truly heard. It's a beautiful gift to give.

Tone the vowel sound "UUH" to balance your root chakra. Take a deep breath and vocalize "UUH" on the exhale. Do this at least three times, getting louder with each tone. This exercise is perfect to do in the morning upon waking to ground and center you.

69

Create a morning ritual. It will consciously connect you with your inner light. Face the sun and bring your hands together in prayer position. Call on the Infinite Light of the Universe to infuse your thoughts, words, and actions. Think about your day and set an Intention for it. Consider adding prayer, toning, or meditation. Begin the day in a beautiful way.

70

Let love be your guide. Not fear. Live with heart, and life will surprise you with possibilities for growth and expansion. Living with heart is the only life worth living.

71

Embrace your inner Kali. Kali is the ancient Hindu Goddess of destruction of the ego. Call upon her when you need to clear yourself of pent-up anger or frustration. Ask her to help you shake, move, or dance it out. Kali can help clear the way, making room for your light to shine.

72

Light a candle and repeat this mantra three times:

I am blessed.

I am free.

Then follow with:

All are blessed.

All are free.

All are blessed.

All are free.

All are blessed.

All are free.

73

Babies are pure bright lights in this world. Hold one. Gaze into his or her eyes. Be dazzled by their light. Looking at a picture of or imagining the face of a smiling baby can work, too.

74

Practice being in the present moment. Don't plan for the future or ruminate over the past, simply *be* in the gift of the present moment. Appreciate what is in front of you. Take in your surroundings and savor the moment.

75

Challenges and pain have value. If we pay attention
to their lessons, they can help us to grow and evolve.
Our light doesn't shun the darkness.

It embraces it and transmutes it into a gift.

76

Delight in the simple things in life. The feel of a cool
breeze on a hot day. The ant determinedly carrying
a leaf on its back. The smile on your child's face. The
sound of a loved one's heartfelt laughter.

77

Practice minimalism. Before you purchase anything, ask yourself if you really need it or if it will truly bring you happiness. Mindless purchases can lead to added burdens and responsibility. Only purchase items and services that will expand your ease, joy, and contribution to the world.

78

Be vulnerable. Share your fears with your partner or loved one. Being vulnerable creates intimacy, which strengthens relationships. Strong relationships are a powerful source of light.

79

Spend time at the beach. Its wide, vast expanse will fill you with a feeling of both peace and possibility and your problems will feel small in comparison.

80

Imagine that you are in a protective golden tube of light that connects you to the Sun and down to the center of Mother Earth. Breathe in the healing, golden energy from the Sun and send that energy to each and every cell in your body. Exhale, and send any negative energy down that golden tube of light all the way to the very core of Mother Earth, where she, the great Recycler, transmutes it into Light.

81

Try this when you have a decision to make. Assign
one answer to your left hand and assign the other
option to your right hand. Imagine your question as
a golden ball of light a couple feet above your head.
Hold your hands palms up at your sides, and ask the
answer to land in one of your hands. Be open and feel
the energy drop into one.

82

Try using flower essences. These ancient healing remedies will raise your vibration, deepen your connection with your spiritual self, and fill you with the particular virtue you need for health and well-being.

83

Take a new route. Take the longer way on the backcountry road. Roll the windows down, feel the fresh air on your face and the wind in your hair. Take a new route and watch for new ideas and inspiration.

84

Make your first thought in the morning a mantra or prayer. Try this one:

Thank you for this day. Thank you for helping me live from my limitless light and helping me fulfill my highest potential in this lifetime.

Create new mantras and prayers and write them down.

85

Go the extra mile. Don't just do what is needed to get a job done, especially for somebody else, and particularly with your work. You'll feel proud and respected, and it will come back to you tenfold.

86

Release your attachment to things and outcomes. Attachment weighs you down and prevents you from being open to new opportunities. Set an intention and then release. Trust the best is on its way.

87

Float.

Float in a river, a lake, or the sea.

Feel the support of the water.

Gaze up into the endless sky.

Feel yourself weightless,

cradled between heaven and earth.

88

Give others a break. We all make mistakes. If you're angry, set a limit to how much time you'll spend being angry. Set a timer for ten minutes and then revisit the situation. Sometimes ten minutes is enough to make room for grace.

89

Rehearse how you'd like a particular meeting or event to go. Visualize the scene in your mind's eye. Use all your senses, and, most importantly, practice feeling the way you want to feel. Whether it's courage, support, or joy, feel what you intend to experience. By rehearsing an important event this way, you cue your subconscious mind and draw your desired outcome to you.

Call upon Archangel Michael for protection and insight. Call his name three times and imagine that he appears surrounded by blue light. Ask him to clear your energy and visualize his sword of blue light slashing away any negative energy. Ask that he seal your aura with his blue flame. Thank him for safeguarding you and helping you to see the Truth of a situation.

91

There is always something to be grateful for. If you're breathing, you can be grateful. Practice gratitude and your life will shift in miraculous ways.

92

Expand your sacral (2nd) chakra. This spiritual energy center governs your emotions, creativity, and sexuality. Visualize a vortex of vibrant orange light a couple inches below your belly button. Take a few deep breaths and imagine the vortex getting bigger and brighter with every breath.

93

Speak up for yourself. Speak calmly and with conviction. Your words, when spoken from a place of awareness, carry light. Let your voice be a light for you and others.

94

Be mindful of how you speak to young people. Speak to them about their strengths, their talents, their potential. They are forming beliefs about themselves and their world that will shape their reality. Give them a head start by affirming the possibilities they hold.

95

Take an Epsom salt bath to clear toxic energy. Salt baths are also a great way to nip a cold in the bud or soothe sore muscles. For extra positive juju, let all the water drain out of the tub before you rinse off and get out.

96

Get a cat. Cuddle with it on your lap. In metaphysical realms, cats are known to transmute heavy energy. Not only do they provide etheric and emotional support, they also contribute to physical well-being. Research shows that a cat's purr can lower your stress level.

97

Take a step every day toward living your purpose, and your life will be filled with meaning, joy, and deep fulfillment. Consistent action, no matter how small, will transform your experience of life from humdrum to hallelujah!

98

Be sensuous.

Add rose petals to your bath.

Wrap yourself in a soft blanket or shawl.

Rub your feet with your favorite oil.

Awaken your senses, and you'll connect with your light.

99

Write a love letter—to God, your Beloved, your child, or to yourself. Read it out loud. There is great power in sending loving words out to the universe. This practice will open your heart and create a sweet treasure to refer back to for years to come.

100

Be with your feelings. If you're angry, punch a pillow. If you're sad, cry. Remember you're *having* a feeling rather than you *are* the feeling. Distinguishing between the two will transform the experience and may bring you a gift of insight or intuition.

101

Visualize yourself as a glorious, luminous sun. Close your eyes and imagine the light shining forth from your heart, radiating out. Notice the strength, the love, and the power that naturally emanate from you.

102

Hum. Proud and out loud or softly to yourself. The sound and vibration creating by humming clears away negative energy. Hum a favorite tune softly while standing in line at the grocery store or loudly while driving or going for a walk. Humming creates good vibrations!

103

Meet your future self. Close your eyes and imagine you're walking on a path in nature. Imagine you meet your future self—the one that exhibits all of the characteristics you'd like to naturally express, the one that has made her dreams come true. Ask her to tell you how she did it. Look into her eyes, receive her energy, wisdom, and love.

104

Go outside and go for a walk or a hike. Moving your body is one of the quickest ways to raise your vibration. A twenty-minute jaunt will lighten your physical, mental, and emotional body!

105

Practice following the Middle Way of Taoism. Chinese Taoists believe that when we embrace detachment and go with the flow, we walk the Middle Way, which promotes inner peace and harmony.

106

Be courageous. Choose courage moment by moment. The word courage comes from the Latin word "cor"—which means heart. Focus on the strength and power of your heart, and you'll overcome your fears.

107

We live in a world of magic and synchronicity. Be on the lookout for signs from your angel guides. Notice the lyrics to songs, the conversations you overhear, your interactions with strangers. They may contain some pearls of wisdom.

108

Smile. Notice the feeling of expansion and optimism it evokes. When you smile, you radiate warmth and love. Acknowledge others when they smile at you. When you appreciate another for their smile and you smile back at them, you magnify the light on the planet.

109

Try something new. Get out of your comfort zone. Take a dance class. Try bungee jumping or sky diving. Do something a little or a lot out of your character. Healthy risks help you grow and evolve.

110

Listen to the communication of your body. How do you feel when you eat certain foods or drink certain beverages? What about when you stay up too late? Or you sit still too long? Pay attention to your body's messages, it wants what's best for you.

111

You are never alone.

You are always connected to the light.

Ask for support.

Ask for guidance.

Ask to grow.

112

Plan a trip. Think of a place that you'd like to visit; research it online or chat with others who have been there. Create a vision board to bring it into reality. Travel not only expands your horizons, it is an opportunity to expand your light.

113

Get excited! Have you ever seen a child get so excited that they jump up and down and squeal with delight? Begin each day with this kind of anticipation. Try it today!

114

Be a steward of the earth.

Plant a tree.

Pick up pieces of trash others have left behind.

Use less electricity.

Recycle.

Eat more plants.

Thank the earth for her beauty, her bounty,
and her regenerative powers.

115

Recite this mantra:

I hold myself and others in high regard.

I cherish life and life cherishes me.

116

Close your eyes and turn your face to the sun.
Feel the sun's rays bathe you in warmth, hope, and
possibility. Breathe in the light.

117

Bid farewell to sugar. Sugar wreaks havoc on your
body and mind. Break up with sugar, and your light
will burn much more steady and bright!

118

Your life is a mirror of your temperament. If you are trusting and proactive, your life will show that. If you are critical and disagreeable, your life will show that. Be mindful of what you reflect into your life.

119

Play with an animal. Throw a ball for a dog. Drag a length of ribbon or string across the floor for a cat. Cuddle your hamster or rabbit or mouse. If you don't have a pet, offer to care for a friend's while they are away or volunteer at a shelter. Spending time with an animal releases stress and brings joy.

120

Create an evening ritual before bed. Light a scented candle and meditate. Read an inspirational book or write in your journal. Take the time to prepare your mind and body for a restful sleep.

121

Speak from your center. Observe your breath. If it's quick and shallow, take a few deep breaths and set an intention to speak from your light. You'll say what you mean with power and compassion.

122

Most people do not get enough touch. Be daring. Instead of handshakes, tell people you're a hugger and ask them if they'd like a hug. You'll be amazed at how many people say yes.

123

Tone the sacred vowel sound for the sacral chakra. Take a deep breath and with the exhale, make the sound "OOO" as softly or as loudly as you like. Set the intention to clear and expand your second chakra. Repeat the tone three times to strengthen your sexual energy and life force.

124

Try this affirmation:

I live from my powerful, radiant light.

I see the world through the lens of my inner light.

I appreciate the light in everything.

125

Watch the sunset. Notice how the light shifts in a beautiful array of colors. Time will slow down and clarity of mind will come. Take comfort that the sun will rise again tomorrow.

126

Call an old friend you haven't talked to in a while. Reminisce over your favorite times together. Friendships keep our light burning bright.

127

Sing alone in the car, in the shower, or in a group with others! Singing is a form of meditation. If you practice harmonizing in a group, the benefits are even more profound.

128

Strengthen your intuition, the voice of your inner Light. Imagine your heart filled with golden light. Imagine that light expanding out until it surrounds your entire body in a golden bubble of light. Sit in this space for a few minutes, then ask your Higher Self for a message.

129

Burn incense. The practice of burning incense is a soothing ritual. Experiment with different kinds: Frankincense, rose, sandalwood, and Nag Champa are all good choices. Burning incense can help clear, beautify, and raise the vibration of a space.

130

Expect good things out of every day and every circumstance. Keep this mindset and you'll be surprised by the new perspectives and opportunities you draw into your life.

131

Practice color therapy. Visualize or incorporate the color gold in your surroundings to increase your self-confidence and motivation. Want to be more creative? Try any shade of green. Need to relax? Visualize a sparkling blue.

132

Practice compassion, most especially toward yourself. When you treat yourself with compassion, you have a solid foundation from which to be authentically compassionate with others.

133

Call upon Archangel Gabriel for guidance about your purpose and your future. In meditation, call her name three times and imagine that she appears with her golden, copper trumpet and surrounds you with a copper light. Ask her for any guidance you need. Answers may come in the form of thoughts or in dreams. Be sure to say "thank you" for her guidance.

134

Sometimes life is hard and cannot be explained.
Accept that there is mystery to life. Challenging
times will bring you to a deeper, richer life expression.

135

Appreciate a full moon.

Get outside and bathe in its light.

Howl at it.

Dance beneath it.

136

Be generous in the giving of yourself. Even if it's just for a moment. Lend a nonjudgmental listening ear, a meal to a homeless person, or spend that extra quality time with your child. It could make all the difference.

Affirm the light in others. Set this intention in the morning when you first wake:

Today I will see the light in everyone.

I will see through the shadows of illusion.

I will see and acknowledge the light.

138

Enhance your intuition by consciously engaging your five senses every day. Listen to the birds, smell the earth after a rainfall, gaze at the stars. Your sixth sense, intuition, will develop and grow.

139

You are blessed and you are loved.

Declare this to yourself as often as you can.

I am blessed and I am loved.

I am blessed and I am loved.

I am blessed and I am loved.

P.S. You are blessed and you are loved.

140

Empty yourself. When you feel overwhelmed, spend a few minutes writing down all of the things in your head. No editing. Just free write. Turn the page and write down some of the things that have made you happy lately. This practice will put things into perspective and makes room for more light.

141

Make delight a priority every day. Live in the moment. Take pleasure in the little things, and you will experience the sweetness of life.

142

Write down your goals. There is great manifestation power in the written word. Write down your goals for the week, for the next month, and the next year. Keep your list somewhere handy and refer to it often to both revise and recommit.

143

Expand your solar plexus (3rd) chakra. This spiritual energy center governs your self-esteem, personal will, and power. To clear and expand your third chakra, visualize a vortex of bright yellow light located a couple inches above your belly button. Take a few deep breaths and imagine the light getting bigger and brighter with every breath.

144

When you witness someone do something extraordinary, courageous, and remarkable, look them in the eye and acknowledge it. Thank them. When you help someone see their radiance, you magnify your own.

145

Talk to a stranger. To the person sitting next to you on the train or in line with you at the store. We need human connection just as we need food and water. It creates community and gives meaning to life.

146

Practice releasing control with a conscious SIGH. A sigh immediately releases tension, regulates your breath, and resets your mind. Take a deep breath and exhale with an audible sigh. Breathe a sigh of relief.

147

Place fresh flowers where you'll see them the most: in the kitchen, on your desk, or in your entryway. Flowers raise your vibration and add beauty to your environment. Flowers are energizing, inspiring, and welcoming.

148

Please don't deprive the world of your light. Don't hide your gifts, your truth, or your authentic expression. Be proud, open, and loving. Shining your light encourages others to do the same.

149

When you have an ache or pain, place your hand over the area. There are energy centers in the palms of your hands. Place your hand over the pain and visualize golden light radiating out from your palm and soothing the hurt. There is healing in your hands.

150

Forgive. Forgive yourself and others. Forgiveness is *for giving*. When you forgive, you give yourself the gift of letting go of the past and starting fresh. Forgive right now.

151

Everyone is a teacher. People come into your life to teach you something. Even if it doesn't appear that way. That person who seems to have everything going for them may be here to fire up your inspiration. That rude or impatient person may be here to teach you to speak your truth with kindness, patience, and compassion.

152

Know that you matter.

You count.

Your very presence makes a difference in the world.

153

Get a massage. Or give a massage. Either will lower the stress hormones in your body and cause the release of oxytocin, the feel-good hormone that opens the heart.

154

Adopt the Hindu greeting, "Namaste." Namaste means, "The divine spark of light within me bows to the divine spark within you." It is often said with a slight bow and with palms and fingers pressed together, upward toward the heart. Whether you say it out loud or silently to yourself, you will connect at a higher level with the person to whom you say it.

155

Find a charity or a cause that inspires you and give to it with your money, your time, and your love. Supporting a charity gives more meaning and fulfillment to your life.

156

Take a sound bath. Use a crystal singing bowl or a brass Tibetan bowl. Hang a wind chime or bells outside your door. Sound can be a gentle, yet powerful way to bring harmony and deep relaxation to the physical, mental, and emotional body.

157

Focus on the golden energy in your heart. This is the center of YOU; the center from which all of your love and power emerges. When you need to move forward with courage, tune in to this energy and affirm the love, light and joy that is your essence.

158

Appreciate the angels in disguise. The person in line ahead of you who paid for your coffee. The person who runs toward danger and helps those in need. The people who meditate, pray for, and take steps to promote world peace every day.

159

Practice the ancient tradition of smudging. Burning sacred herbs, such as sage, helps clear out stagnant or negative energy. Walk around and hold the smudge stick at knee or waist level as smoke travels up. Keep at least one window or door open for ventilation. Hold the intention to clear and release energy that doesn't serve you.

160

Go out in the rain without an umbrella.

Get wet.

Splash in puddles.

Or sing and dance in it like Gene Kelly.

Rain is a blessing, a cleansing, a renewal of life.

161

When you're feeling down, look at photographs. Doing so will remind you of all the good and connection you have in your life. Reminiscing helps you realize how rich and abundant your life truly is.

162

Listen to your gut—your deep inner feelings. These feelings come from your soul, which knows best. Trust your gut.

163

Keep your flame burning bright. Saying "yes" when you want to say "no" doesn't serve anyone. Setting boundaries is one of the best ways to take care of yourself. Conserve your light.

164

Step into your True Self. Become the bright light that you truly are. The world needs you. All you need to do is take the next step.

165

Act as if you are already what you most desire to be. If it is your dream to be a writer or an entrepreneur or a yoga instructor, ask yourself, "How would I live this day (as a writer, an entrepreneur, or a yoga instructor)?" It's inspiring! It will encourage you to start living your dream.

166

Pay it forward. Pay the toll for the car behind you. Share the time left on the parking meter with another driver. Write a positive review online for a product or service you purchased. Be the pebble in that pond that starts the ripple effect.

167

Go easy on caffeine. A little is ok, but consider sipping on dandelion leaf or peppermint tea for an invigorating, body-nourishing alternative that will help you shine bright.

168

Observe silence. Stop, close your eyes, and simply breathe. Do nothing. Release thought. Try to slip into silence when you need to inject a moment of peace and calm into your day.

169

Are you just coasting through life? Are there passions you're not pursuing because of fear? Take a courageous step toward the fulfillment of your heart's desires. That's why you're here.

170

Tone the sacred vowel sound for the solar plexus chakra. Take a deep breath and with the exhale, make the sound "OHH." Repeat the tone at least three times to increase your confidence and align your personal will with Divine Will or your Higher Self.

171

Daydream. Go ahead, it's good for you! Daydreaming puts your left-brained thinking, planning mind on the back burner and allows the creativity of your right brain to have its way. Many of the greatest ideas, from the best artists and scientists in history, have emerged from daydreaming.

172

Be open to love. When your heart is open, everything is more sweet and gentle. The Universe is benevolent. Love is always available to you.

173

Eat lots of raw organic fruits and vegetables. Fruits and vegetables are nourished by light and water. Eat from the full color spectrum of the rainbow for maximum radiance. Go raw. Grow brighter.

174

Don't let other's opinions guide your life.

Know yourself.

Trust yourself.

Be your own guide.

Your light will show you the way.

175

Practice tension and release. Lie down and tense every muscle in your body that you can as tightly as you can for five seconds, then relax. Repeat this exercise two more times. The process of contracting and relaxing your muscles brings immediate physical, mental, and emotional relief.

176

Don't put people into boxes. When you categorize people, you reduce them and close yourself off to what could be a meaningful connection. Give people a chance.

Create an evening self-care ritual. Make it special. Enjoy a cup of herbal tea. Wash with your favorite lavender soap. Moisturize your skin. Try a natural toothpaste with fennel or clove. Place your hands on your heart, look in the mirror, and feel gratitude for your beautiful body.

178

Censor yourself. When you get together with
a friend, fight the urge to dump your problems
on them. It is human nature to connect through
suffering, yet it is also nourishing and wise to connect
through joy. Share your tribulations succinctly. Share
your stories of success, however small they may be,
with lots of detail.

179

Dance. Every day. Alone or in a group. Dancing is an expression of your light. It's a fun way to exercise, and it opens your channel to the divine.

180

Try aromatherapy. Add lavender oil to your bath for deeper relaxation or dab peppermint oil on your temples to ease a headache or boost energy. Diffuse eucalyptus oil if you have a head cold. Aromatherapy is powerful physical, mental, and emotional medicine.

181

Before tackling your To Do list, ask your heart in which order you should proceed. This is especially important on your days off. Do the things your heart yearns to do *first*, and you'll accomplish the other tasks with more ease and harmony.

182

Be yourself.

You are a treasure to the world.

If you weren't, you wouldn't be here.

183

Call upon Archangel Raphael for the healing of your body, mind, and spirit. In meditation, call upon him by saying his name three times. Ask him to surround you with his emerald green light. This light will clear your energy, help you heal, and bring you peace. Make sure to say "thank you" for his healing power.

184

Go outside and appreciate the sky. Think about all of the beauty you've seen play out in its expanse—beautiful sunsets, wispy clouds on a sunny day, dramatic thunderstorms, the starlight of the night sky. The sky is a canvas of light.

185

Focus on the flame of a white candle. The color white evokes purity and illumination. Ask the flame to melt away any sadness or unwanted energy you may be carrying. Ask it to help you expand your awareness of your light.

186

Sit next to a river, creek, or brook. Or consider adding a small water feature in your home. The sound of flowing water will calm and soothe your emotions and promote mental clarity and creativity.

187

In the shower, imagine that you are standing under a huge waterfall of love and light. Feel the light enter your body and soothe and relax every muscle, fiber, and cell of your being. Let it wash away any energetic debris or negative thoughts you don't wish to carry anymore. Bathe in the Light.

188

Take a slow, deep breath as you count to five. Breathe all the way down into your belly. As your breath reaches your belly, imagine a small flame being lit there. Hold for a count of five. Then slowly exhale through your mouth to a count of five. Do three rounds of this deep breathing, feeling the warmth in your belly expand, then ask your Inner Light what it wants you to most be aware of in this moment.

189

Create a list of things you love. Read it back to yourself and feel how much you appreciate everything. Keep it handy for those moments when you've forgotten your natural inner radiance. It will light you up and help you attract more of what you love into your life.

190

Appreciate your food. Thank it for increasing your radiance as it travels through your body. Bless it and all those who grew, handled, and prepared it.

191

You are a radiant being of light and love. You don't need to do anything to prove your worth. You deserve to live your dreams because you are here!

192

Take a luxurious bubble bath. Try some natural scented bubble bath like lavender, chamomile, or rose. Feel how weightless your body feels in the water. Allow the warmth of the water to soothe and relax you.

193

You cannot control the weather, but you can always make the sun shine inside your heart. Bring your hands into a prayer position, take a deep breath and think of something for which you are grateful. The clouds will lift and you'll feel your optimism break through.

194

Unplug from social media. Stay away for a day, maybe a weekend, or even a week. Make plans for dinner with friends, host a gathering, take a class or an experiential workshop. Be with people in real life.

195

All remarkable, wise people have been put through the ringer of life in one way or another. If you feel you've been put through the ringer, see it as a springboard for your eventual greatness to be shared with the world.

Expand your heart (4th) chakra. This spiritual energy center located at your heart governs your ability to give and receive love. To clear and expand your fourth chakra, visualize a beautiful vortex of emerald green light there. Take a few deep breaths and imagine the vortex getting bigger and brighter with every breath.

197

Practice mindfulness. Throughout the day, stop what you're doing and notice what you see, what you hear, what you smell, what you feel. Let the beauty of the present moment enter your heart. Let the light in.

198

Remember: the world and everyone in it is your mirror. When you see things you don't like, ask yourself, "How am I like that in my life?" Sometimes we strongly dislike a trait in somebody else when we are like that ourselves, or when we could really use *some* of it ourselves. Somebody's rude behavior toward you could be a sign to speak up for yourself.

199

Practice "Aloha." In the Hawaiian Huna tradition, saying "Aloha" is not only a greeting of love, it is a way of life. Aloha is being a part of all, and all being a part of you. Your pain is my pain. Your joy is my joy. Respect is given to all as part of the Creator, and no one and nothing is ever willfully harmed. The earth, the sea, and the sky are ours to care for and cherish. Aloha.

200

Practice *deliberate* acts of kindness. Smile at strangers. Call clerks by their names. Hold the door open for people. When you are deliberately kind to others, it creates a domino effect where they then are kind to others too.

201

You are a bright light.

You shine.

You are loved.

Shine on.

202

Run warm water over your feet. Either while lying in the bath or under the hose on a warm day. Imagine that the water is sacred, a blessing. Imagine the water baptizing you into a higher level of spiritual awareness. Feel yourself cleansed and sanctified.

203

Play with a dog. Their sweet, unconditional, loving nature will heal your heart. Or go to a dog park and enjoy the spontaneous fun and exuberance of these joyful creatures!

204

Reduce. Reuse. Recycle.

Do your part.

Try composting.

Carry a grocery tote bag.

Grow an edible landscape.

Let's lighten up the planet.

Revere Mother Earth's heart.

205

When you're tired, rest. Take an afternoon cat nap. Think of it as a sacred duty rather than a luxury you can't afford.

206

Your inner Light speaks to you through your intuition. It may sound like your own voice spoken softly and confidently, or it may speak to you in the form of images. Trust it and follow through. The more you flex your intuitive muscle, the stronger it will grow.

207

Don't limit your radiant self-expression. When you're happy, jumping up and down or skipping down the street are fine options. Joy is contagious. Share it!

208

Wear natural fabrics, such as cotton and silk. Natural fibers feel good on the skin and help your body breathe. Go natural; enhance your radiance.

209

Hand your worries over to your angels. Visualize yourself handing them a black box, and as they receive it, picture it dissolving into sparkling light. Feel the relief. Feel your heart open. Give gratitude.

210

Become super aware of your immediate surroundings. Look at something in front of you, to either side of you, and behind you. Look, listen. Take in the details. Awareness brings you into the present moment and into a state of appreciation.

211

Enjoy yourself today. Make a mental or written note of at least one thing you will do today that will leave you tickled pink. Take half an hour to read a book, go on a short hike and pick some wildflowers, or meet a friend for tea. At the end of the day, revel at the delight you created.

212

Try incorporating some superfoods into your diet. Wheatgrass is high in chlorophyll, a powerful antioxidant. Tumeric is high in curcumin, a powerful anti-inflammatory, and chia seeds are high in omega-3s, a powerful brain booster. Try some superfood and boost your super power.

When practicing manifestation, imagine the quality your desire will give you as opposed to the specific desire itself. For example, imagine what prosperity and fulfilled purpose feel like as opposed to focusing on a particular job or imagine what love and intimacy feel like rather than focusing on a particular person. The universe may manifest these qualities in ways that you might not have ever imagined.

214

Give yourself permission to have a good cry. Listen to
some cello or other piece of classical music to assist
you. Have your tissues ready. This release of energy
is so cleansing for your body and soul. Let your tears
flow and have faith that the best is yet to come.

215

Honor your inner "YES!" Only move forward with something or someone when you intuitively feel a powerful "YES." If it's an "I'm not sure," or a "Well, kind of," wait. That's your inner light's way of saying there's a much better option. Trust and wait for your inner "YES!"

216

Honor the Sacred Masculine within. This energy is pure, powerful, and protective. It is the guardian of the womb of creation. It takes a stand, yet fights only for love. It initiates action with integrity, wisdom, and courage. Honor the Sacred Masculine energy within to live fearlessly, passionately, and wisely.

217

When you feel fear, don't be trapped by it. Shake it out. Move it out of your body and then focus on your heart, where your inner Light lives. Let your heart motivate and inspire you toward your fullest expression.

218

Send a handwritten note to someone you think might need it. A simple expression of your love and gratitude for them is enough to lift someone's heart.

219

Spend time with young children. Young children haven't been programmed by society yet, so they are closer to the veil and more in touch with their light. Ask them questions as if you were speaking with a wise being. You are.

220

Practice this visualization: Picture someone you love. Really see them in your mind's eye. Now imagine them smiling at you. When you feel yourself physically begin to smile, send them a blessing of appreciation and love.

221

Tone the sacred vowel sound for the heart chakra. Take a deep breath and with the exhale, make the sound "AHH". Set the intention to clear and expand your fourth chakra. Repeat the tone at least three times to help enhance your ability to both give and receive love.

222

Practice this popular Tibetan Buddhist mantra: "Om Mani Padme Hum." Phonetically pronounced: Ohm Mah Nee Pahd May Hum. Whether spoken out loud or silently to yourself, this mantra will invoke the loving and unconditional nature of compassion within you.

223

You are a spiritual being of light having a physical experience. Your life is part of your eternal journey. Breathe this awareness into your body, the temple of your soul. Be an embodiment of light.

224

Whenever you are missing a deceased friend, family member, or pet, recall a moment of joy that you shared with them. Step back into that memory's feeling, and set the intention to send them love. They have passed onto a higher frequency, so you will be far more able to feel their love via the energy of your remembered joy, rather than sorrow. Try it.

225

Write yourself short uplifting notes. Put one on your fridge. Tape one to your bathroom mirror. Tuck one into your wallet and in the sun visor of your car.

226

Let your past go.

Forgive yourself.

Brush yourself off and step into the Now.

227

Do something you loved doing when you were a kid. Collect rocks from a stream. Run under the sprinkler. Have a talent show. Doing the things you loved as a kid will keep your sense of wonder alive. Stay young at heart.

228

Bake yourself or a loved one a sweet treat, from scratch. Baking is an outlet for creative expression and it's a sweet way to express your love!

229

When in doubt, do nothing.
Rest ... Trust ... Receive.

230

Do some form of meditation daily, whether it's observing your thought, your breath, or visualizing your inner light. With regular practice, you'll be able to stay centered in the midst of chaos and confusion. Meditate. Be a warrior of light.

231

Live with authenticity and speak your truth. Those who are not in alignment with your virtues will fade from your life and your relationships will be rooted in mutual support and love.

232

Step out of yourself and into the world. Look up! Notice the sky, the birds, and the trees. Keeping your focus up lightens you up.

233

Take a twenty-minute sound-healing stroll. Go for a walk, ideally in nature, and with every slow, deep breath, exhale with the soft releasing sound of "Uhhh," which helps release stress and negativity. On your way back, exhale with the sacred vowel sound "Ahhh," which raises your vibration and centers you in your heart. A sound-healing stroll is a fun and powerful form of a walking meditation.

234

If it feels like your heart is breaking, let it. That's how the light gets in. When we let go of the controls and confines we've placed around our heart, it has room to breathe and grow.

235

If you have a chronic pain or disease, try this practice: Ask your angels to surround you in a bubble of golden light. Then ask your body to share any messages that lie underneath the physical manifestation. Feelings may come up. Let them. Follow any insights revealed.

236

Listen to the laughter and play of children. Their pure, innocent joy is one of the highest vibrations on the planet. Their spontaneity and freedom of expression will fill you with light.

Practice gratitude every day. Focusing on what you are grateful for will draw more of that to you. Express gratitude affirmatively: "I'm grateful for my health and peace of mind," rather than "I'm so grateful I'm not sick and stressed out." Your subconscious, your great reality generator, responds better to words spoken in the affirmative.

238

Thoughts lead to emotions. Emotions form vibrations within your body and the universe. Your thoughts hold great power. Remember you are blessed with the power to change them whenever you like.

239

Try on compassion when you feel least able. That guy cutting you off in traffic may be rushing to the hospital for an emergency. He probably needs your blessings. Hold compassion for yourself, too. That mistake you made at work was an honest one, and you learned a valuable lesson.

240

Get grounded every day. Stomp your feet. Place your palms on the earth. Stand in Mountain Pose. You cannot bring the dreams of your mind and heart into reality without being fully grounded.

241

Honor an ancestor today. Light a candle for a loved one who has passed on. Give gratitude and appreciation for all that they were to you in life. Send them a blessing of peace and love.

242

It's not only OK to dance to the beat of your own drum, it's what you're meant to do. Find your rhythm and dance.

243

Give someone a blessing. Offer them a blessing of what it is you think they need or what you're lacking yourself. You can do it silently or out loud.

May you be blessed with love, abundance, and joy.

244

Smile for a minute. For an entire sixty seconds. This is fun to experiment with when you're feeling sad, angry, or frustrated. Smiling for an entire minute will cue your subconscious that there are things to be happy about. Smile for a minute. Smile awhile.

245

Try to eat more vegetarian and vegan meals. You will not only improve the welfare of our sentient friends, you will help heal your own body and the planet. You'll also help keep your intuitive channels clear.

246

Music has the power to shift your vibration quickly. Listen to music that makes you feel good. If you feel angry or anxious, listen to raucous music to help move it out of your body. If you need to cry, listen to a moving classical piece. Follow up with listening to sounds of nature, harp, or chimes to make you feel calm and centered.

247

Call upon Archangel Uriel to illuminate your mind with information, wisdom, and insight. In meditation, call upon him by saying his name three times and imagine that he appears and surrounds you with his yellow light. Make sure to say "thank you" and continue to see yourself surrounded by his yellow light for as long as you need to receive the information you need.

248

Watch the delight of a child experiencing something new for the first time. See their eyes light up with wonder. Listen to their spontaneous expressions of curiosity and joy. Feel their excitement!

249

Let your light guide your actions moment to moment, not the pings and dings of your phone and computer. You don't need to answer every voicemail, email, or text right away, if at all. Check in with your light before you check in with your devices.

250

Expand your throat (5th) chakra. This spiritual energy center governs your communication and creativity. To open, clear, and expand your fifth chakra, visualize a vortex of rich blue light at your throat. Take a few deep breaths and imagine the vortex getting bigger and brighter with every breath.

251

Be YOU. Don't try to be somebody else you admire. Let that person inspire you to be a better you . . . the BEST you . . . but uniquely, completely, holy YOU.

252

If you're not feeling well, imagine taking a leisurely stroll through one of your favorite places in nature. Use all of your senses. See the rich green of the grassy meadow, the vibrant colors of the wildflowers. Smell the fresh summer air. Hear the soft breeze rustling through the trees. Let the power of your imagination take you there.

253

Keep a journal. Writing about your feelings can be a powerful way to process emotions and gain clarity. Don't just list your complaints and worries. Remember to record the moments that touched your heart and the people that brought beauty to your life.

254

Let go of the little things.

Let go of the big things.

Let go and give it all to God.

255

Find a form of exercise that you enjoy and do it regularly. Walking, dancing, yoga, tennis, running, strength training; or throwing a ball, jumping rope, or playing hopscotch with your kids! Keep moving, and you keep moving forward.

256

You are adored. Yes, ADORED. Get quiet enough, and you will hear the universal choir of angels singing of their love and adoration for YOU!

257

Practice soul gazing. Sit facing a partner, palms up. Gaze into each other's eyes. Imagine a circular stream of golden or pink light flowing between your hearts with your breath. As you inhale, imagine breathing in their light energy. As you exhale, send them your own.

258

Tread a little lighter on Mother Earth. Take public transportation today if you can, or walk or ride your bike. When we tread lighter, we commit to keeping the planet beautiful for our children.

259

There is a reason we are called human *beings* and not human *doings*. Realize your goals of BEING: Be courageous. Be compassionate. Be creative. Be of service. Be you.

260

Imagine what your relationships would be like if you chose to accept your loved ones exactly as they are now. Give up the idea that your mate will be great once he or she learns this or does that. Realize that your child is different than you are. This is loving unconditionally, a love that heals all.

261

Toss worry out the window. Instead of focusing on what you don't want to happen, focus on what you DO want to happen. You can always affect change, no matter where you are now. Hold the goal as your vision, feel it, and let your light be your guide.

262

Your imagination is one of your most powerful, God-given vibrational tools. Use it to imagine yourself, your life, and your world as you'd like it to be. Use your imagination to complete the sentence, "Wouldn't it be lovely if . . . ?" and then take one small step toward fulfilling that creative vision.

263

Make your bedroom a sanctuary. Remove the TV, the computer, and the phone. Keep it tidy. This space is the last thing you see before you close your eyes and the first thing you see when you open them in the morning. Making your bedroom a tranquil place will help you sleep soundly and wake peacefully.

264

Travel.

To another city, another state, or another country.

Immerse yourself in the experience of another place.

It's interesting, fun, and highlights our shared humanity.

265

Give of your light freely, without expectation. The universe is always exchanging energy. When you give of your light freely, it will be reflected back to you like a prism, in infinite ways!

266

You possess the courage to be the bright, shining light that you are.

You were born with it. Fan the flame with your attention and action. Stoke your inner fire.

267

People's differences and eccentricities are the treasures of our collective humanity. We're ALL oddballs in one way or another. It's what makes life interesting. Vive la Difference!

268

Meditate on your connection to All That Is. Visualize your energy as golden light radiating out from your heart. Visualize it spiraling out to the world in a beam of positivity. Feel the golden light coming back to you in return. Feel the universal love that connects us all.

269

Be someone's cheerleader. Encourage them to be themselves and to utilize all of the gifts they've been given. Go team Light!

270

Celebrate the resilience of nature. Admire the persistence of the little weeds poking up in the cracks of the sidewalk and the tenacity of the trees lining the busy freeways. We, too, can adapt and persist.

271

Sing these famous song lyrics by Harry Dixon Loes
for an immediate lift:

"This little light of mine, I'm gonna let it shine.

This little light of mine, I'm gonna let it shine.

This little light of mine, I'm gonna let it shine.

Let it shine, let it shine, let it shine!"

272

Use discretion. Discretion is the freedom to decide what is right in a given situation. It's a way of tuning in before acting out. Exercising discretion keeps you on the path of grace.

273

Speak out. Speak about what you are *for* rather than what you are against. Stand for peace instead of being antiwar. Your voice matters. Your words are powerful.

274

Set an intention for your life. Intend to be an embodiment of peace, compassion, or joy. Consider your goals through the lens of your intention. They may shift or come more clearly into focus. Intention is the seed of creation.

275

Tone the sacred vowel sound for the throat chakra. Take a deep breath and with the exhale, make the sound "EYE." Set the intention to clear and expand your fifth chakra. Repeat the tone at least three times to help speak your truth, set boundaries, and express your creativity.

276

Simplify. Get rid of what you don't need or what doesn't give you joy. Donate the items to your local homeless or women's shelter. Lightening your load will lighten your life.

277

Magnificent things can come from small beginnings.
Contemplate the mighty oak that began as an acorn
or the radiant sunflower that began as a seed. The
same potential for growth is in you. What will you
become?

278

Pray. For yourself. For others. For the world. Pray for
those you'd rather not pray for. There is great power
in prayer. Pray with others. Pray alone. Pray like every
day is a day of Thanksgiving. . . . It is.

279

Mahalo. "Mahalo" means thank you, but it is an expression of gratitude as a way of life. Make mahalo your mantra during the good, the bad, and the absurd. Thank the universe in advance for the growth that comes from every situation, even though you may not see it.

280

Practice this meditation: Imagine holding the earth in the palms of your hands, surrounding it with brilliant, golden light. Visualize the light infusing the entire planet and every being upon it with peace and love. Send the whole world light.

281

When you point a finger at someone, there are
three fingers pointing back at you. How or where in
your life might you be the very way you're accusing
another person of being? Own the disowned parts of
yourself that you project onto others.

282

Stretch your body *and* your mind. An open mind that
seeks understanding is a conduit of light.

283

Try a juice fast or a cleanse. Research and speak with your doctor, naturopath, or holistic health practitioner for guidance beforehand. A cleanse can help your physical, emotional, and spiritual body feel lighter.

284

Sing to someone or something you love. Singing raises your vibration. It makes no difference if it's for your friend, your fish, or your ficus.

285

Lean in. Lean into your fears, your vulnerability, and your uncomfortable feelings. If you lean in and express yourself, your self-esteem and confidence will grow. You may find that you're supported, encouraged, and celebrated.

286

Create an emotional vision board. Fill it with photos that depict feelings you'd like to experience in your life, such as joy, peace, prosperity, love, and fulfillment. Place it where you will see it every day. Holding a vision for your life will help make it a reality.

287

Ask for sweetness in your life. Your energy will soften just by asking. You'll feel much more appreciation for the little things: your pet's greeting, the daisies reaching for the afternoon sun, the smiles of people you come across. The world is full of sweetness.

288

The next time you're in an elevator or close confines, connect with the people there with you. Break the awkward silence and say "hi." Ask them how they're doing. Pay them a compliment. Simple exchanges like this connect us to humanity.

289

Create your own purpose mantra. Try: "I am a radiant being of light. I inspire others to know and live by their own light."

290

Seek your own counsel. What would your inner light do? Instead of asking everybody else's opinion, ask your light and trust the answers given.

291

Remember that everybody is doing the best they can
with what they've been given. Even you. Trust in that.

292

Don't be attached to the source of your joy or the
source of your love. This will only bring you pain.
Trust in the universe, and your life will overflow with
delight.

293

Get up early and watch the sun rise. Try it, even if you're not a morning person. Watching a sunrise fills you with feelings of peace, optimism, and inspiration. Witnessing an event that occurs every day, most times without notice, affirms life and your place in it.

294

Honor yourself. If something doesn't feel good, walk away or say "no." Honor your authentic responses to life, and your light will SHINE.

295

If you find yourself in a spiral of negative thought,
call on your Higher Self or your angel guides to
infuse your thoughts with divine truth and wisdom.

296

Allow yourself to lie down and rest. Imagine that you
are floating on a billowy, white cloud in a clear, blue
sky. Feel your body become weightless like the cloud.
Allow it to release any tensions and anxieties you may
be carrying.

Call upon Archangel Zadkiel to help forgive yourself and others. He radiates compassion and love. In meditation, call upon him by saying his name three times and imagine that he appears to you surrounded by a violet light. Make sure to say "thank you" and continue to see yourself surrounded by his violet light for as long as you need.

298

When you experience physical pain, take slow breaths and with each exhalation, visualize the pain as a river, flowing down through your feet and leaving your body. Imagine it streaming into the ground, where it is absorbed by Mother Earth and transmuted into Light.

299

Spend time in nature as often as you can. If it's not possible, listen to recordings of the sounds of nature indoors: a babbling brook, ocean waves, birds. The sounds of nature will help balance your nervous system, release feel-good hormones, and lower your heart rate. You will love it and your pets will too.

300

Expand your third eye (6th) chakra. This spiritual
energy center located between the eyebrows governs
your insight and psychic abilities. To clear and
expand your sixth chakra, visualize a vortex of indigo
light there. Take a few deep breaths and imagine the
light getting bigger and brighter with every breath.

301

Accept people as they are, where they're at. Just do it. When you accept people, they will either fade from your life or rise to the occasion. There is great alchemical power in acceptance.

302

Trust in the process of your life. Trust even when something doesn't go the way you'd planned. Experiencing unrequited love? Didn't get the job? Remember, rejection is God's protection. Have faith that a better romantic partner or job is on its way.

303

Avoid making any big decisions when you are upset. Shake it off, dance, meditate, or take a nap and then decide. Your decision will be made from your True Self, which is where the best decisions arise.

304

Visualize the light in your heart. See it expand beyond your body, your home, your city, your country and then beyond planet Earth and out into the galaxy. From this place of infinite light, set an intention. Be open to miracles.

305

Attend a drum circle or try drumming. If you don't have a drum, any percussion instrument or surface will do. Drumming is powerful. It inspires expressive, creative, and vibrant energy within you. It lowers stress and improves mood. Find the rhythm inside you!

306

Pay attention to your self-talk. Ignore the voices in your head telling you that you aren't enough. Wrap your arms around yourself and give yourself a squeeze. Look in the mirror and acknowledge how unique, extraordinary, and amazing you are.

307

Give someone a hug. Hugging is good medicine. It transfers positive energy and communicates on a soul level. Give a hug and receive one in return.

308

Dive into your uncomfortable feelings. Gently and compassionately explore them. Trust that the benevolent universe is trying to tell you something. Simply sit, feel, and listen. Uncomfortable feelings usually arise because we are attached to an idea of how things should be. When you conduct a gentle, direct inquiry, your heart opens and you come home to yourself.

309

Believe in yourself and in your dreams. Your dreams were placed in your heart to be fulfilled. They are an expression of your Light. You hold the power to manifest them. Live your dream!

310

To activate your manifestation power, act as if you already are the person you dream of being. Be courageous, be self-expressed, be calm, be compassionate. When you "act as if," you will soon see how much you already are the person you dream of being.

311

Treasure elders. They offer wisdom and insight from years of living. Ask them for advice. Invite them to tell their stories. Their faces will light up. A relationship with an elder can inspire and enrich your life.

312

Make sure to get a good night's sleep. At least seven hours. Eight or nine if you can. We heal our bodies and minds while we sleep. Your light needs good rest to keep shining bright.

313

Go with the flow. If your day isn't going your way, surrender. Be curious and look for the gift that the situation holds. There is a treasure hiding there somewhere. You may get a sweet surprise or the gift of insight, knowledge, or truth.

314

Eat your favorite food on occasion. Appreciate how it looks, smells, and feels in your mouth. Indulge yourself in the experience. Enjoying a meal is one of the small pleasures in life. Savor each bite.

315

Treat everyone you see and interact with as though
they are an expression of God, Source, the One Love
(they are). You'll regard people in a more honorable,
purposeful, and loving way. Your exchanges will be
rich and meaningful. Your life will be more rich and
meaningful.

316

Share in creation. Plant a garden, complete a big
jigsaw puzzle, build a tower of blocks. Invite others to
join you. Creating something with others brings you
closer to them. It creates meaningful connection. It
creates light.

317

Remember, it is your perception of the world that determines your experience of it. You are free to perceive as you wish. Choose to see through the eyes of empowerment, beauty, and love.

318

Go easy on yourself. When you are easy with yourself, the world is a softer, more graceful, and pleasant place.

319

Be someone's angel. Don't just be a witness to an injustice, do something about it. If you witness someone being harassed, engage the victim in a casual discussion about the weather or pay them a few compliments. Ignore the aggressor. This is usually all it takes. Don't let an uncomfortable situation discourage you from your light.

320

My grandfather often said, "You just can't get there from here."

Sometimes you need to put the brakes on and find a new route. Tell your ego to take a back seat and let your inner light steer you to the right track.

321

Appreciate others.

Tell them.

Be generous.

Don't keep it to yourself.

We all want and need to be valued.

322

Try practicing yoga. This ancient system of balancing body, mind, and soul comes in many different styles and forms. A regular yoga practice releases toxins and stress from the body, promotes physical health, and enhances mental clarity and feelings of well-being.

323

Give your cares to Mother Earth. When you're
feeling low, lay belly down on the ground. Imagine
all of your worries pouring into Mother Earth, who
will transform them into Light. Thank her for her
nourishing, loving support.

324

You are unique and your unique YOU is needed
on the planet. Somebody out there will benefit
immensely from your unique smile or laugh. Without
your special Being-ness, life's rich human rainbow
wouldn't be complete.

325

Tone the sacred vowel sound for the third eye (6th) chakra. Take a deep breath and with the exhale, make the sound "AAA". Set the intention to clear and expand your sixth chakra. Repeat the tone at least three times to help create a clear vision for your life as well as to increase your intuitive abilities.

326

Seek the inherent wisdom in nature. Nature stands the test of time. It adapts, perseveres, and grows despite oftentimes harsh conditions. There is community in that redwood tree grove. There is longevity in that cluster of ancient boulders. Look to nature, and you'll likely find the clarity you seek.

327

Find three things to be grateful for at the end of the day. Even when it's hard, you can still find things to appreciate in your life. Write them down in a journal or on slips of paper you add to a jar. The cumulative effect of this practice is powerful. Cultivate an attitude of gratitude.

328

Fill your heart with so much love and appreciation that there's room for nothing else. Choose love.

329

Watch the birds. Whether you go on a bird watch or observe them in the park or from your window, spend some time watching our feathered friends. Birds are a delight to see and hear. They bring grace and beauty to our surroundings. Watch the birds, and your soul will spread its wings and take flight.

330

Be true to yourself while being compassionate with others. If you ignore your heart's desires, you enervate your soul. Be true to yourself, be honest with others, be empowered to shine bright.

331

Enjoy the journey. Don't focus on the destination.
The journey is an opportunity for adventure,
discovery, and connection. There's light in each step.

332

Learn to both give and receive compliments. When
giving a compliment, be authentic and specific.
When receiving a compliment, simply say, "Thank
you." Giving and receiving compliments with grace
magnifies the light inside you and the light inside
others.

333

True spirituality is an energy of inclusivity. Our very essence is love, an endless love for all. Exclusivity resides only in the minds of men, not in the heart of God.

334

Choose at least one night a week to enjoy a meal with your family. Prepare, cook, and eat the meal together. This is a nourishing way to bond with those closest to you.

335

"EEEE" is the sacred vowel sound for the crown (7th) chakra. Take a deep breath and exhale in the highest pitch tone you can make. Don't strain. Practice and find the tone that you can sustain with ease. This exercise connects you to Source and opens a channel for energy, guidance, and love to flow.

336

Watch one of your favorite movies. Whether it's a comedy or a drama, escaping the real world for a couple of hours can nourish your body, mind, and spirit. Watching the hero's journey play out in a story can inspire you to overcome your own challenges and be the hero in your own life.

337

Hold your head high.

You are a radiant, beautiful being of light.

Don't let anything eclipse your light.

338

We have three brains: A head brain, a heart brain, and a gut brain. Tune into your head for information, tune into your heart for truth, and tune into your gut for intuition. Use this combined intelligence to live with light.

339

Swing on a park swing or in a hammock. This playful act is one of life's simple pleasures. The feeling of your body gliding rhythmically through the air will fill you with exhilaration and delight.

340

Call upon Archangel Jophiel to help you see the beauty already present in your life, to help you with any creative project, or to help you bring organization into your home or office. In meditation, call upon her by saying her name three times and ask that she surround you with her deep fuchsia light. Make sure to thank her for her gift of inspiration, motivation, and clarity.

341

Be artistic. Purchase a set of pastels, watercolors, or colored pencils and a sketch pad. Sketch, paint, or doodle. Focus on the fun and not the outcome. Unleash your inner artist to express him- or herself without judgment from your ego. Finding time to be artistic fosters creativity in other aspects of your life.

342

Incorporate dry skin brushing in your morning routine. Before you take a shower, brush your skin with a firm, natural brush. Start at your hands or feet and brush towards your heart, using small strokes. Dry skin brushing is an ancient technique for cleansing the body inside and out. It keeps you glowing.

343

Try this creative work break. Go outside, stretch your arms overhead and imagine that you can breathe in the energy of the sky. Take a deep breath and as you do, imagine that you are breathing in its limitless positive possibilities.

344

Be willing to face your shadow self. Your shadow self is all of the repressed and undesired aspects of your personality stored in your unconscious mind. Explore those parts of yourself you work to contain. Ask your shadow what it needs from you. Attending to your dark side helps you to evolve, to live more in your light.

345

Use candlelight in the evenings from time to time. The soft glow of candlelight has lit the night for thousands of years. It inspires intimacy and promotes a feeling of peace. Candlelight is sacred, reverent, holy light.

346

No matter what has happened to you or what you have or haven't done, you deserve to be happy and make your positive contribution to the world.

347

Practice patience. Look to nature as your guide. Flowers take time to bloom. You can't force anyone or anything to bloom. Divine timing rules your affairs. There is no need to rush.

348

Try alternative giving during the holiday season. Tell your friends and family you will donate to charity on their behalf and ask them to do the same. Alternative giving is a gift of light. A gift that makes a difference.

349

Go outside and appreciate the night sky. Contemplate its vast darkness. It will clear your mind and invite opportunity for introspection. Spend time star gazing. You are made of stardust. Make a wish upon the brightest star you see.

350

Ask the universe for a gift today. Ask for a sweet gift (best not to be specific). You'll be amazed at what shows up!

351

Expand your crown chakra. This spiritual energy center located at the top of your head governs your connection with the Universe, your higher power, your inner light. To clear and expand your seventh chakra, visualize a vortex of white or violet light facing up toward the heavens. Take a few deep breaths and imagine the light growing bigger and brighter with every breath.

352

Speak with authority and conviction, or be quiet.
There is great wisdom and illumination in both.
Sometimes things are better left unsaid. Ask your
inner light which is best.

353

It is before the dawn that the sky seems the darkest.
Oftentimes things seem to be at their worst the
moment before they get better. Have faith. Believe in
the Universe and yourself.

354

Compassion for others = give others a break. Put yourself in their shoes. Compassion for self = speak up for yourself and set boundaries. Living this balance is living your light.

355

When you experience emotional pain, call one thing to mind that you really like—an animal, a flower, a place—then take the time, whether in person or in your imagination, to be with that one thing. Feel the velvet muzzle, the soft petals, or the fresh air. If you stay focused on that one thing that makes you happy, you will feel lighter inside within minutes.

356

Words are powerful. Our experiences are affected by our language. Watch your words, and watch your life transform.

357

Listen to the sound of crystal singing bowls. The resonant sound penetrates the body and is deeply relaxing. The tones anchor high frequencies, which help you become centered in your light.

358

Please don't judge others.

You haven't walked in their shoes.

They don't need your condemnation.

They need your prayers of strength and love.

359

Become acquainted with a flower. Get right up close and take it in. Notice the vibrancy of its color, the beauty of its design and fragrance. Flowers are powerhouses of light.

360

Give yourself permission to grieve. On your own time. Amidst your grief, give yourself permission to appreciate the myriad blessings and beauty you have despite your loss. Grief is a passage. Take all the time you need.

361

Meditate with crystals. Try clear quartz crystal for clarity or rose quartz for self-love. Selenite and hematite will help clear negative energy. Cleanse your crystals by placing them in the sun for a day or under the moonlight for a night. Crystals are conduits of light.

362

Remember that before you came into your body, you were a magnificent spiritual being of light. Affirm the Eternal Truth of who you are every day. Hourly if necessary.

363

Let the tenderness and grace of your light heal your "should-haves," "could-haves," and "wish I would-haves."

364

Join or create a Heart Circle. A Heart Circle is a group of people who come together to share their feelings. Everyone listens without interruption. You can ask for input, but you are never told what to do. Heart Circles are safe, nurturing keepers of light.

365

When something comes to an end, whether it's a project, a relationship, or a chapter in your life, take the time to honor it. What wisdom did you gain? What can you be grateful for? How did your heart open? Did the light get in? Remember, as one door closes, another opens. Step through the door, centered in your light.

Acknowledgments

I am profoundly humbled and honored to be in a position to share 365 ways with the world to spread light. My gratitude to the Infinite Creator—the One Light—is never ending.

Special acknowledgment goes out to all of my guides and comrades on the angelic realm who helped me write this and whose perspective, wisdom, love, and humor both astound and delight me every day.

I'm deeply grateful to Christine LeBlond, my editor, whose suggestions and edits made this book a more accessible and richer experience for everyone who reads and practices it. Namaste! Special thanks also to my agent, Krista Goering, as well as to all of the wonderful team at Red Wheel Weiser/ Conari Press.

Thank you to my beloved family, extended family, and friends—especially my beautiful sister, Christine, as well as my dear friends Casey, Cheri, Noel, Suzie, and Viola, for their passionate minds, laughter, and love.

I'm also in deep appreciation for the works of Dr. John Demartini, Adyashanti, Rev. Michael Beckwith, Derek Rydall, David Hawkins, Rick Moss, Gangaji, Abraham-Hicks, Les Brown, and Landmark Education. Each has affected me in powerful, positive ways just when I needed it most.

And "thank you" can't encompass the depth of joy, love, and gratitude I have for my Beloved—Nate Jensen—whose heart, passion, and commitment to art and life as art, has sparked a wildfire in my heart, helping me to shine more brightly. Thank you, baby, for your contribution to the cover of this book and to my life.

About the Author

Mikaela Jones has been studying, practicing, and teaching various forms of meditation, hypnotherapy, spiritual empowerment, and New Thought disciplines for over twenty years. She is a sound healer, offering both individual and group sound-bath meditations through the Portland Sound Sanctuary, a group she co-created in Portland, Oregon. Mikaela is an intuitive and the author of *The Little Book of Light: One Hundred Eleven Ways to Bring Light into Your Life*. It is her deepest prayer that her work will help you more deeply connect with your True Self, allowing you to overcome adversity and shine your Light with the world.

Visit her at *www.MikaelaJones.com*.

To Our Readers

Conari Press, an imprint of Red Wheel/Weiser, publishes books on topics ranging from spirituality, personal growth, and relationships to women's issues, parenting, and social issues. Our mission is to publish quality books that will make a difference in people's lives—how we feel about ourselves and how we relate to one another. We value integrity, compassion, and receptivity, both in the books we publish and in the way we do business.

Our readers are our most important resource, and we appreciate your input, suggestions, and ideas about what you would like to see published.

Visit our website at *www.redwheelweiser.com* to learn about our upcoming books and free downloads, and be sure to go to *www.redwheelweiser.com/newsletter* to sign up for newsletters and exclusive offers.

You can also contact us at *info@rwwbooks.com*.

Conari Press
an imprint of Red Wheel/Weiser, LLC
65 Parker Street, Suite 7
Newburyport, MA 01950
www.redwheelweiser.com